P9-DEZ-479

Class Meetings

Young Children Solving Problems Together

Emily Vance and Patricia Jiménez Weaver

An NAEYC Comprehensive Membership Benefit

National Association for the Education of Young Children
Washington, D.C.

Photographs © copyright by
Emily Vance and Dani Schwartz, pp. viii, 10, 26, 28, 31, 46, 52, 62; Eva Anthony,
front cover/center; Jean-Claude Lejeune, front cover/top left and bottom right,
p. 39, back cover; Elaine M. Ward, p. 54; and Marilyn Nolt, p. 66.

Much of the material in this book is based on *Class Meetings and More!*
by Emily Vance and Patricia Jiménez Weaver, published by Tortuga Press, Tucson,
Arizona, in 1995. For more information on class meetings, check author Emily
Vance's Website at **www.classmeetings.com**

National Association for the Education of Young Children
1509 16th Street, NW
Washington, DC 20036-1426
202-232-8777 or 800-424-2460
www.naeyc.org

Through its publications program the National Association for the Education of
Young Children (NAEYC) provides a forum for discussion of major issues and
ideas in the early childhood field, with the hope of provoking thought and promoting professional growth. The views expressed or implied are not necessarily those
of the Association. NAEYC thanks the authors, who donated much time and effort
to develop this book as a contribution to the profession.

Library of Congress Control Number 2002114639
ISBN 1-928896-07-3
NAEYC Product #222

Publications Editor: Carol Copple
Associate Editor: Catherine Cauman
Design and Production: Malini Dominey

Printed in the United States of America

About the Authors

Emily Vance holds a master's degree in elementary education from the University of Arizona and a Child Development Associate credential. She teaches at a Reggio Emilia-inspired preschool in San Diego, California. In her more than 30 years of experience in the field of early childhood education, Emily has found class meetings to be a powerful approach to student problem solving and classroom management. Since 1995 she has been a consultant to other educators about class meetings, and she has made a number of award-winning children's videos. Emily is pictured on pages viii and 52.

Patricia Jiménez Weaver has taught children grades K–5 from culturally diverse backgrounds using developmentally appropriate practices for more than 28 years. She is a curriculum specialist in an inner-city elementary school in Tucson, Arizona. Patricia co-authored an article on mathematics for *Instructor Magazine* and has presented at local, state, and national conferences on innovative teaching methods related to literacy, math, science, and class meetings.

Acknowledgments

As authors we would like to acknowledge our students. Without them we would not be the facilitators we are today. As with any new approach, trial and error are the keys to learning and development. We appreciate our students' patience throughout this process. They have taught us that we can trust them to find solutions to their problems, thus making this world a better place to live. They have opened our eyes to the understanding that their problems can be solved in a variety of ways without depending on adults to create solutions that may or may not make sense to them. Our students have surprised us with their unique ways to solve problems.

We would also like to acknowledge our families, Jason, Jessica, John, Juan Tomás, Carlos, and Aaron, for their support.

A special thank you to principal Rosanna Gallagher for encouraging us to use class meetings; Suzanne Sheard for sharing this approach with us; and Pauline Baker, Sylvia Chard, Cecilia Chavarin, Lisa Clifford, Sheldon Koester, Carolyn Marsden, Cecilia Perez, Lori Fraesdorf-Peth, and Jay and Gail Rochlin.

A Word from the Authors

This book is written *by* teachers, *for* teachers. Too often education programs are developed by noneducators who have not considered all of the dynamics of using their methods in a school setting over a long period of time. The programs may look good in theory but prove difficult in practice.

The program presented here we have used in our classrooms over a period of years and found to be practical and effective. We outline concept, guidelines, and examples from our practice. You know your children better than we do—use your own good judgment in adapting and applying these ideas.

We offer this word of advice about beginning to use the approach to class meetings described in this volume: such meetings are not something you try once a week for a few weeks and then decide whether they are working. We recommend that teachers use this approach regularly for at least three months. This gives the teachers time to gain a level of comfort and skill in facilitating the meetings and gives the children time to become familiar with the routines and processes involved. Further, teachers will have the opportunity to observe the effects of class meetings on the classroom climate and interactions. As with all good classroom management programs, patience, commitment, and consistency nurture long-term results.

In our experience, teachers become believers in class meetings when they see children beginning to use problem-solving strategies *outside* the meetings, depending less on adults, and using positive language with each other—stepping-stones on the path to healthy self-esteem and respect for others. Class meetings help create a safe environment for everyone. These elements are key in turning a group of individual children into a real community of learners.

Chapter 1

What Are
Class Meetings?

One October morning Angelina comes to me in tears. Someone has gone into her cubby and eaten the special Halloween cupcake she brought for lunch. She cannot believe anyone would do such a thing. I suggest discussing the problem in class meeting later that morning.

During class meeting I invite Angelina to share her problem. "My mother bought my sisters and me Halloween cupcakes. I saved mine for lunch today. But someone went in my cubby and ate my cupcake. Look, here's all that's left!" She holds up the torn wrapper. The children's faces show deep concern. They appear shocked at the idea of someone going into another's cubby without permission.

"Angelina," I ask, "Do you know who was involved in this problem?" She doesn't. Although I have an idea who it might be, it is important for the class to come up with the information themselves.

At this point Jennie raises her hand: "I saw Roberto over by Angelina's cubby." Several children confirm this observation.

I ask Roberto if he knows anything about the problem, and he nods, adding, "Luis was there too." Luis says, "So was Ben." I thank the three boys for their honesty and ask them if they are willing to help find a solution. They all say yes. I acknowledge their cooperation.

"Angelina, do you have any ideas about how to solve this problem?" I ask. Angelina shakes her head. "Roberto, do you?"

"Shake hands," Roberto suggests.

I ask Angelina if this is a reasonable solution. She says, "No, that's not going to solve my problem."

Next I turn to Luis. "Luis, do you have an idea?"

"Say sorry," Luis replies.

Angelina is unequivocal in her response to this suggestion: "That won't solve my problem or bring back my cupcake."

"Ben, how about you? Any idea how to help Angelina with the problem?" Ben looks down at the floor and shakes his head.

Damien raises his hand: "I think Roberto and Luis and Ben should bring in some money to pay for the cupcake."

Ian adds, "Yeah, if they each give Angelina a quarter she can buy a new one."

I ask Angelina if she feels this is a reasonble solution, and she says yes. I ask Roberto, Luis, and Ben if they are willing to go along with it, and they all agree to.

Angelina goes to lunch with a smile on her face.

Imagine how you would feel if someone went into your cubby without your permission and ate the special treat your mother had sent you for lunch. How would your anger and disappointment affect your ability to concentrate? If you were given an opportunity to talk to the person who did it—to share your feelings, hear that person's response, and arrive at a solution—consider the difference it would make in your day.

Class meetings have a positive effect on the school day. They offer a forum for group problem solving, with the children solving the problems and the teacher facilitating. They provide an opportunity for everyone to speak out about their feelings in a nonthreatening environment, where thoughts and views can be expressed without fear of ridicule, finger-pointing, or recriminations. They help make school a place that is emotionally safe for children. This feeling of safety enhances children's ability to concentrate and learn.

This is how Gail McClurg explains to her kindergartners the concept of class meeting (which she calls community meeting):

> I introduce it very simply as a time when we can talk about our lives together in such a way that everyone can feel safe and have a chance to speak about the things on our minds. When there is a problem, we can help each other look for a solution.
> I make it clear as the first meetings proceed that this is a time to problem solve, not to judge. We really need to listen to each other, and everyone is important. (1998, 31)

During class meeting a child who needs help resolving a conflict presents her view of the problem. The other children involved in the incident give their perspectives. With guidance from the teacher and suggestions from the rest of the class, the children involved work out a

A father writes: "In our American judicial system and on our playgrounds, conflicts are resolved using an adversarial model. The class meeting goes beyond the idea of winners and losers, victims and perpetrators, and moves to the realm of solutions, cooperation, and community."

solution they can all accept. From their experiences in class meetings, children learn that honesty is valued, feelings are respected, and classmates care about each other.

Creating a sense of community

Respect is key in ensuring a safe, positive environment in class meetings—and in the classroom and school settings. It is the foundation upon which a caring atmosphere is built. The teacher communicates its importance through her words and actions. An adult's first step toward creating a respectful classroom is modeling respect in her own interactions with the children. (See Pauline Baker's approach in "Starting with Respect," pp. 6–7.) When the teacher models openness, empathy, and thoughtfulness in helping children resolve their differences, even very young children begin to learn to settle their problems respectfully.

Discussing the value of class meetings, Donna Styles (2001) writes,

> Class meetings unify the class—as conflicts in the class are resolved and feelings are shared, friction is reduced. At this point, the class begins to function as a community, working together toward goals and showing support for all members. Students feel a sense of belonging to the group, and the tone in the classroom becomes very positive and caring. (p. 9)

The format of class meetings and the sense of community the meetings foster encourage a number of prosocial behaviors. In meetings children learn to take turns and listen respectfully. As they hear and consider others' perspectives, children become more capable of seeing beyond their own egocentric view of situations. They learn to empathize. Recognizing and expressing appreciation for others' constructive actions is another benefit, enhancing each child's social competence while fostering a positive climate in the group. Finally, children learn to evaluate ideas and decide on reasonable, respectful solutions. Learning to solve problems and resolve conflicts in the group, children bring this experience with them and use it in their daily interactions.

Promoting cognitive development

Even beyond the interpersonal arena, class meeting time is valuable for children's learning and cognitive development. To describe a problem situation to the rest of the group and the teacher, the child is called on to recall events in sequence. He has to put into words what he recalls, enhancing his language skills. William Glasser adds,

> Another advantage of class meetings is the confidence that a child gains when he states his opinion before a group. In life there are many opportunities to speak for oneself. The more we teach children to speak clearly and thoughtfully, the better we prepare them for life. When a child can speak satisfactorily for himself, he gains a confidence that is hard to shake. (1969, 144)

Listening and trying to understand what happened—often from two or more perspectives—all the children use and extend their receptive language skills. Because children are typically quite interested in problems brought to class meeting, they struggle to comprehend what is said and to envision the events they hear described.

A parent observes: "At the class meetings I've seen, the children clearly demonstrated that rather than one or two, there might be four or six or seven points of view, all valid, that describe a given event. Once those points of view were understood, the children seemed prepared to move on to solutions and finally actions."

Starting with Respect

What values and beliefs do we communicate when we deal with conflicts between children? Our every thought, action, and conversation communicates our values in an early childhood program. When you as the teacher make a conscious, thoughtful effort to create a climate in which respect influences every interaction, children will learn to work together in collaboration. In such an environment children can begin to learn problem-solving skills even when they are too young to participate in a formal class meeting.

When faced with a conflict between children, try to respond calmly to the problem. Express your sincere concern for the sadness, anger, or hurt that you see, and your desire to find ways to respond to these feelings. You may want to calm the children down by taking some deep breaths together.

Be sure the children involved are near enough for you to listen without distractions. Sometimes you and the children may need to move to a quieter location before beginning a dialogue about the problem. Let them know that you want them to work this out together so that the next time they encounter a problem, they will have ways to solve it.

Listen carefully as the children tell you what they think happened to cause their conflict. They are offering you a part of who they are and what they understand about life and living. Many influences have shaped their experiences and thus their ability to deal with conflict. You cannot change these things, but you can help children learn respectful ways to respond to conflicts.

When each of the children has had an opportunity to give a perspective on what happened, invite them to contribute ways to respond to the feelings expressed and to work toward a solution. Listen carefully and allow the children time to respond. This effort will involve your being open to the many ways children communicate. Words are only one means to communicate feelings and respond to problems. You can gain information by paying attention to the children's facial expressions and body language.

As you speak and interact with the children and develop solutions, remember to think about the messages your body is sending as well. Are your eyes focused on the children? Are you listening with your whole body? Are you relaxed and open to the possibilities that children bring to such an important effort?

Children need guidance and patience when learning strategies for solving problems in respectful ways. Even if a child immediately says she's sorry, try to continue the dialogue to keep the problem from recurring. "I'm sorry" has become a quick fix children use instead of developing positive ways of interacting.

Let each occasion to negotiate and collaborate be a time when you remind the children of their capacity to solve problems. Reflect on the decisions and refine them to fit new moments. In this way a strong foundation is created.

Teaching is an art. Every day you and the children are creating beauty. Offer children the tools, materials, and opportunities to create their own solutions to the inevitable conflicts that arise in life. There are no easy answers or prescriptive steps to handling conflicts, but there is an easy rule to remember every time you are confronted with a problem:

Start with respect.

Pauline Baker, who contributed this piece, is the studio art teacher at a Reggio Emilia-inspired state-funded preschool in Tucson, Arizona. She has also served as a resource teacher and child development college instructor.

These highly engaging experiences with language and interaction are very useful to children learning a second language. Moreover, both language comprehension and formation of internal representations of things and events (often from written or spoken words) are critical skills throughout schooling. Beyond these vital capabilities, class meeting challenges children to practice and extend other higher-order thinking skills, such as

- drawing on long-term memory,
- brainstorming possible solutions,
- using analytical thinking,
- evaluating solutions from various perspectives, and
- putting together these steps in problem solving.

Fostering skills for life

Class meetings are beneficial for all age groups, from preschool through kindergarten and the primary grades. In school, in play, and at home, children draw upon the social skills and cognitive learning honed in class meetings. Problem solving, strategizing, negotiating, analyzing, speaking in a group, appreciating other perspectives—when these skills are introduced early in life and reinforced in kindergarten and the primary years, children internalize them for use throughout the life span. They are abilities valued not only in the school setting but also later in the workplace and in adults' personal interactions and relationships.

Rheta DeVries and Lawrence Kohlberg place the importance of class meeting—its role in building a caring community by developing

In the words of a primary school administrator: "We would be remiss not to make experiences like class meeting a daily part of the total learning program. These children leave our classrooms equipped with options, tools, and strategies for coping with social situations, as well as with academics. Our students' futures—personal and professional—will be more successful as a result of acquiring these social skills."

cognitive abilities and promoting strong social skills and values—at a higher level, outside the classroom setting and in the larger society:

> By building a just community, teachers are engaged in the most important task of education: helping children develop the intellectual, social, and moral competence, the "habits of thought and action," on which the survival of social democracy and individual human welfare so vitally depend. (1990, 181)

Chapter 2

The Nuts and Bolts

C ircle time, gathering time, morning meeting, community meeting—class meetings have many different names and take just as many forms. Meetings may tie in to specific aspects of the curriculum or offer community-building activities or routines to ease young children's daily transitions from home to school. Although our class meetings have features touching on all these themes, the focus in this book is on problem solving and making the classroom a safe, positive environment so that children can channel their energy into constructive interactions and learning.

These next pages explain the four major components of class meeting in our classroom—opening, acknowledgments, problem solving, and closing. However, teachers need not adhere rigidly to our format or routines. They can use them as a starting point or borrow and adapt elements to fit their classroom needs and the needs of their children.

Opening class meetings

The teacher calls the children together for class meeting, inviting them to form a circle so that each child can see everyone else. First or second graders may prefer to place their chairs in a circle, while younger children can sit on the floor. In our preschool program the children range in age from 3 to 5 years. If they're engaged in activities in the classroom, I call them together with a song:

> *Come and join us on the rug, it's gathering time [clap, clap]*
> *Come and join us on the rug, it's gathering time [clap, clap]*
> *Come and join us on the rug,*
> *Come and join us on the rug,*
> *Come and join us on the rug, it's gathering time. [clap, clap]*
> (Sing to the tune of "If You're Happy and You Know It.")

When the children are playing outdoors, we call "Gathering time!" and they take up the cry, passing along the message and heading inside at a run. Class meeting quickly becomes a favorite period. Class meetings can open with a familiar song or the same song every day, then move on to a brief activity or game, such as finger plays for children who are younger, to help them come together as a group. Teresa Harris and Diane Fuqua tell us,

> This is a time for shared rituals that give children meaning as a specific, special group of people. Gathering together is a time to acknowledge the unique contributions of each member of the

group. Predictable routines and rituals also provide structure for the day ahead and offer a sense of safety, belonging, and caring for one another. (2000, 44)

Meeting openings are a transition time. Their purpose is to bring the children together and to help them let go of stressful feelings, tension, and worries so they can concentrate on the day's activities and learning. From time to time we begin the meeting with a special activity. Children talk about others who are on their minds—someone who is sick; a family member, friend, or classmate whom they miss; perhaps a pet. The children pretend to place their special names in the center of the circle. Then we all hold hands and send love and kind thoughts to those who have been named in the circle that day. By sharing each other's concerns and loving thoughts, children draw closer together as a community.

Acknowledgments

The acknowledgments portion of class meetings encourages children to notice others' positive actions and voice their appreciation for another person's thoughtfulness, assistance, or courtesy. Acknowledgments are not to be confused with compliments. An acknowledgment recognizes a meaningful interaction between people, whereas a compliment is a flattering observation about another person. When a teacher uses an acknowledgment, such as "You and Jimmy played together for a long time at the sand table," instead of the standard classroom phrasing, "I like the way you played with Jimmy today," she is recognizing the child's positive behavior rather than praising

A teacher says:
"The most important part of class meeting is the acknowledgment of appropriate behavior by the children. In my bilingual, multiage classroom, I have seen children acknowledge appropriate behavior in many instances outside the format of class meetings. I have heard children praise and acknowledge as well as voice their own needs to one another."

him for pleasing her. Acknowledgments provide information without being manipulative or controlling. (See "Giving Children Useful Feedback.")

Acknowledgments quickly become a crucial part of our classroom life. Children do not naturally seem to notice others' constructive actions. Like empathy, sharing, turn taking, and other social skills,

Giving Children Useful Feedback

As early childhood teachers, we continually give children feedback. We need to make sure that we do so in ways that are respectful and productive. In recent decades, researchers and expert practitioners have warned against praise that tends to undermine a child's intrinsic motivation—that is, the child's acting for motives or rewards within himself (Brophy 1981; Stipek 1998; Kohn 1999). *Evaluative praise*, such as "Good job" or "You're a really great helper," leads children to look for external proof that they are good or right (Moorman 2001). When teachers make frequent use of evaluative praise with children, they actually may cause children anxiety: If the teacher can give, the teacher can also take away (Moorman 2001).

Descriptive feedback, by contrast, notes specifically what children do. A teacher might say, "I noticed the three of you worked together at the computers today" or "Look, the ball went farther when you threw it with one hand." Such feedback helps children focus on what is relevant to the task or situation and not on winning praise from the adult.

Another kind of positive feedback is acknowledgment or *appreciative praise* (Moorman 2001), which often includes the words "I appreciate" or "thank you." For example, a teacher might say to a young child, "Thanks for cleaning up the block area. You've helped get our classroom ready for tomorrow."

recognizing and acknowledging others for their positive actions is a skill that must be learned. Once our children pick up this skill, we hear acknowledgments given freely in the classroom and on the playground. Acknowledgments have made a dramatic difference in our classroom climate. And appreciating the positive in situations or people is a habit of mind that works to an individual's advantage throughout life.

Children may acknowledge other children or teachers. Their contributions vary, depending on their age and the level of their communication skills. For instance, Jamal, a kindergartner, raised his hand and said, "I want to acknowledge Tiffany for helping me clean up the blocks." Tiffany said, "Thank you, Jamal," letting him know she appreciated the acknowledgment. Eli, a sixth grader, said, "Thank you, Mrs. Deal, for helping me with my long division." Georgina, a second grader, said, "I want to acknowledge Antonio for helping me write the word *job* in my journal," and Antonio thanked Georgina for the acknowledgment.

After acknowledgments we move to problem solving, the heart of class meeting. Because our preschool has such a wide age range, at this point in the meeting the youngest children in our group—the 3-year-olds—leave with another teacher. Class meetings that work for 4s and 5s can be too long for very young children to sit through. (For problem-solving strategies with this younger age group, see "Negotiation Chairs" in Chapter 4, p. 53.)

Problem solving

The problems most commonly brought to class meetings are interpersonal, especially name-calling, arguments or disagreements, and taking someone's property without permission. Many other interpersonal problems come up regularly—excluding others from play, not taking turns or sharing, and aggressive or bullying behavior, to name a few. When a child brings a problem to a meeting, the first step is gathering information.

In gathering information, all perspectives on an incident are heard and considered, not just the view of the child raising the issue. The children take turns presenting their views—everyone involved will have a chance to speak. The teacher makes this clear, often repeating this point to reassure children who interrupt that they will have a turn soon but must listen in the meantime. Children who witnessed the incident contribute their views. Problems are discussed without accusation or judgment, with those involved taking responsibility for their actions and earnestly seeking a solution.

Few people are born with the ability to consider problems fairly and constructively. It is a skill children can acquire over time through daily practice in a respectful and caring environment, under the attentive guidance of a patient teacher. Gradually children learn that "the purpose of all discussion is to solve problems, not to find fault or to punish. Experience in solving social problems in a non-fault-finding, nonpunitive atmosphere gives children confidence in themselves as

rom a -year-old boy who is a two-year veteran of class meetings: " henever imon does something bad or a few kids aren t following directions, the new teacher makes all of us sit □uietly with our hands folded. It isn t fair, and it doesn t make imon or the other kids do better the ne□t time. he never even tries class meetings."

thinking, worthwhile people" (Glasser 1969, 129). The ultimate goal is for children to internalize problem-solving techniques so they become second nature. Then as problems occur throughout the day, children can deal with the problems themselves, without the intervention of an adult. (See "Resolving Conflicts without Adults," p. 18)

The child presenting the problem explains her view of the situation. For example, Gabriella, a first grader, says, "My problem is that Rosa calls me names. It makes me feel bad." The teacher asks Gabriella what steps she took to resolve the issue herself—did she talk to Rosa? Gabriella says, "I asked her to stop, but she didn't." What happened next? "When she didn't stop, I moved to another part of the playground. Then I signed up for class meeting." The teacher then asks Rosa if she remembers the incident.

Early in the school year, before the concept of the classroom as a safe environment has been well established, some children may hesitate to talk about their part in a problem for fear they will be reprimanded or punished. They may shy away from answering a question or they may not answer honestly. If Rosa says she remembers the incident, the teacher immediately commends her for her honesty and acknowledges her willingness to help resolve the issue. If Rosa does not remember, the teacher goes back to Gabriella for more information, perhaps asking her when and where the incident occurred.

At this point other classmates will wave their hands in the air, saying, "I saw it. I know about this problem." The teacher can get the perspectives of these bystanders as well. However, it is important that the attention stay focused on Gabriella and Rosa, the children directly involved in the problem. The problem is theirs, and discussion and resolution will be most meaningful coming from

Resolving Conflicts without Adults

Children can use four problem-solving steps to attempt to clear up misunderstandings. These steps encourage children to communicate respectfully with each other outside the formal structure of meetings. In many cases they will find that they can reach an agreement without teacher guidance.

Often a problem can be cleared up when the child in distress uses the first two strategies:

1. Calm down; take some deep breaths.

**2. Talk to the person with whom you are having a problem.
Use I-feel statements.**

This is the preeminent problem-solving strategy employed in class meetings. (See "Learning to Use I-Feel Statements" in Chapter 3, p. 40) Respectful communication is the social skill the teacher fosters when he intercedes in children's disagreements in the classroom or on the playground and when he guides problem solving in meetings. Helping children internalize modes of respectful interaction is key. If talking is not productive, the child can take the next step:

3. Move away from the other person.

This should end the disagreement—at least for the moment. (Not all problems need be resolved. Some just naturally fade with the passage of time.) If these strategies fail to provide relief, and the child wants to pursue a solution, he can

4. Sign up for class meeting.

Over the course of the school year, through purposeful teacher prompts and the use of teachable moments, these steps will become second nature to children, providing a strong foundation in conflict resolution that they can use throughout life.

them. (In "An Unwelcome Kiss," pp. 20–21, classmates seek clarification and make contributions during the problem-solving process.)

After the circumstances have been clarified, the teacher asks the child presenting the problem to propose a solution. A solution is acceptable only if all children directly involved in the problem agree to it. For example, Gabriella might ask Rosa to give her a hug or to draw a picture for her. If Rosa agrees, Gabriella says, "My problem is solved." If not, the teacher can ask Rosa to propose a solution. If necessary, she can invite the children in the class to contribute their thoughts. This is a good time for the teacher to reiterate to the children that solutions must be reasonable, respectful, and related to the problem at hand.

Not surprisingly, in a class meeting children may arrive at a solution or strategy that does not actually solve the problem back in the classroom or on the playground. Of course the teacher keeps an eye on how things turn out. If all goes well, she may remark to the children about how well their solution worked out. And if things do not go well, the teacher can consider various options when the problem arises again. Sometimes she will do some on-the-spot problem solving with the children directly involved. In some cases, the teacher may feel that the whole group could benefit from hearing what happened and doing some thinking about a solution more effective than the one first tried.

Some issues raised in class meetings are not conflicts at all. Sometimes children bring up unfair situations. Some situations may occur in school (see "Cristi's Library Dilemma," p. 23). In other cases children are concerned about out-of-school problems: "The sidewalk's all broken; that's why Lucy fell down. We've got to fix the sidewalk so kids don't get hurt" (Pelo & Davidson 2000, 40). Such concerns call for

The Nuts and Bolts

the same kinds of problem-solving skills that children develop in class meetings focusing on conflicts. And when a class meeting becomes a forum for addressing an unfair situation, it fosters the group's consciousness about the welfare of others. With guidance,

An Unwelcome Kiss

Liliana has a disagreement on the playground with Daniel, a child from a class that does not hold class meetings. Liliana signs up for class meeting.

When Daniel comes to our classroom for the meeting, I describe our meeting procedures. I tell him how the children involved in a problem explain their views of it. I take extra time to emphasize that each person has a chance to explain what happened without being interrupted.

Liliana speaks first. She says Daniel kissed her on the head and kicked her while they were on the slide. Daniel interrupts Liliana several times, and each time I reassure him that he will have an opportunity to talk.

When it is Daniel's turn to give his view of the incident, he says, "Liliana asked me what I wanted to play. We decided to play chase on the slide. After playing chase for a while, I decided I didn't want to play it anymore, so I pretended to kiss her." Daniel explains he pretended to kiss Liliana by blowing a kiss at her. "Then Liliana hit me with her elbows. So I kicked her."

I thank Daniel for being honest and giving us the information we need. I tell him that by doing so, he lets us know that he is willing to solve the problem. At this point it's important to allow time for children's questions so everyone understands what happened.

Eleni: Liliana, did you hit Daniel?

Liliana: Yes.

children feel empowered to address the inequity, to work toward righting the wrong.

As teachers we should keep in mind that not all problems need to be solved. Sometimes children just need to talk about a situation and have

Eleni: Daniel, did you kick Liliana?
Daniel: Yes. She hit me.
Valerie: Liliana, why did you hit Daniel?
Liliana: Because he kissed me.
Alberto: Daniel, did you try to kiss Liliana?
Daniel: Yes, but it wasn't a real kiss.

After these and other questions are answered, the children offer a number of possible solutions:

1. Liliana and Daniel should play away from each other.
2. Liliana and Daniel should shake hands and say sorry.
3. Liliana and Daniel can play on the same side of the playground but not on the same equipment.
4. Daniel should tell Liliana when he doesn't want to play anymore instead of pretending to kiss her.
5. Daniel shouldn't pretend to kiss Liliana.

Liliana and Daniel agree to use solutions 2 and 4 to settle their disagreement. They feel that solution 2 will remind them that they are still friends and solution 4 will help prevent the problem from happening again.

When someone from another class takes part in problem solving, it confirms for children the importance of class meeting and validates their ability to resolve conflicts.

their feelings acknowledged. Children need to be heard. McClurg gives this example from a meeting in her kindergarten:

> Brant complained about having a small part in *Jack and the Beanstalk.* Two of his classmates expressed similar disappointment: one said he'd had a hard time accepting the role of the cow, and the other said he'd do his best although his part was small. Brant was able to see that he was not the only one experiencing disappointment, and I had an opportunity to reassure the children that I was keeping track so that eventually everyone would get a major role in one of our plays. (1998, 31)

Closing the meeting

After one or two problems are resolved, it is time to close the meeting. The teacher might close by acknowledging a student, saying something like, "Juanita, thank you for sharing your idea for solving Jaime's problem today." Or she may want to close the meeting by having the children sing a song or play a game.

Another way to close is to ask the children if anyone solved a problem without the help of adults. Adila, a kindergartner with a year's worth of class meeting experience, recounted this success story:

> "One time I was outside and I wanted to play with Safina, Maria, and Solidad. I asked them if I could play with them, and they wouldn't let me. So I went to get Raoul and Maria's older sister Angela to help me. They said some stuff in Spanish to the girls. Then I got to play. I felt good because I got to play and I got my problem solved without any grownups."

This is an effective way to motivate children to carry out beyond the classroom the strategies they learned in class meetings.

Cristi's Library Dilemma

Every day the first graders visit the school library. They are divided into four groups, each with a different color library card: red, blue, green, or yellow. To check out books the children place their cards in the appropriate color-coded pocket on a pocket chart. When children are responsible for the checkout procedure, they tend to be more conscientious about it. However, many children forget to return their books the next day.

To help children remember to return their books daily, the school librarian devises an incentive: If everyone in a color group brings back their books three days in a row, each group member can check out a special book bag containing a stuffed animal and a book. Upon hearing this, the children's eyes light up.

Within two weeks, a pattern emerges. All the children in the yellow group return their books consistently and take home the special book bags. None of the children in the other three groups get the book bags.

One day in class meeting, Cristi raises her hand: "I want the kids in my group to remember to bring their books back so we can check out book bags too." Cristi reminds all of the children in the red group to return their books. A few days later, when she realizes her reminder is not working, she suggests to her group that they leave the books in their cubbies overnight so that they will be sure to have them to check in at the library the next day. Not all of the children cooperate. Finally, Cristi brings up the problem again in a class meeting.

Cristi says, "I don't think this is fair. I return my book every day, but because others in my group don't remember, I can't check out a book bag."

I ask Cristi if she would like to talk over this problem with the librarian. She says yes and leaves the meeting to go to the library immediately.

When the librarian hears Cristi's dilemma, she sees the problem and changes the system. As a result, Cristi takes home a book bag regularly.

Finding time

Teachers new to the concept of class meetings may feel they barely have time in their busy classroom schedules to cover the curriculum let alone hold daily meetings. However, class meetings create more time for learning rather than using up learning time.

When two children are arguing in a classroom where the children participate in class meetings, the teacher can intervene without disrupting the learning: "Leroy and Elise, I see that you are arguing. You seem to have a problem. Would you agree to put your problem aside for now, and we will discuss it and try to resolve it later in class meeting?"

When children know they will have an opportunity to redress their grievances later in the day, they are able to temporarily set aside their worries and concentrate on learning. The time saved in not stopping to sort out conflicts during classroom activities and learning more than makes up for the time spent in meetings:

> Over time, children will begin to care for one another, solve their own problems, feel more empowered and more in control of their learning, and come to view all in the community as their "teachers." It will be time well spent. (Harris & Fuqua 2000, 47)

Does this mean that teachers should hold class meetings only when children have a problem? (See "What If We Don't Have a Problem?") We started out that way but soon learned that it is best to meet regularly—ideally on a daily basis. More frequent meetings enable children to practice their problem-solving skills and address issues before they snowball.

If you are just beginning to use class meetings and are weighing the benefits, make a commitment to hold them for at least three months

What If We Don't Have a Problem?

Class meetings are not just for problem solving. They teach respectful communication and foster social skills and cognitive skills. Teachers can use the problem-solving segment to talk about group projects, have small groups work on math or science problems, prepare for a field trip, or teach a song related to the curriculum. (See Chapter 4, "Variations.")

You may want to compile a list of Things to Discuss When We Don't Have Problems. Here is a sampling of ours:

1. How can we get the block area picked up quickly?
2. Do you have to clean in a place where you did not play?
3. What makes a friend?
4. Do you always do what your friends tell you to do?
5. What happens if we step on a book?
6. What is your favorite color [or food or animal]?

before judging the results. It may take that long for children to incorporate their new social skills, begin to use them regularly, and learn to trust one another. The change in the classroom's social climate will be noticeable.

Many teachers use class meeting times for group learning. Meetings work well for group discussion of, say, math or science problems. By working together in a group, young children learn that there is more than one approach to solving a math problem. (See Sylvia Chard's section on class meetings and the project method, pp. 56–60 in Chapter 4, for more on this topic.) Glasser states,

There is no reason that teachers cannot use [class meetings] for arithmetic, history, science, and other subjects. Whole-class teaching reduces isolation and failure. . . . The team, for example, is the basis of competitive athletics. But in the class curriculum, where it could be equally effective, it is little used. By treating the whole class as a unit, the same spirit of cooperation can arise as arises on athletic teams. (1969, 143–44)

Class meetings may be as brief as 10 minutes or as long as 30 minutes, depending on the children's ages, the amount of business at hand, the nature of the meeting, and the scheduling demands for the day. Children age 5 and older can come together once a day for a more sustained period of 20 to 30 minutes. For preschoolers, we recommend holding two short class meetings, each 10 to 15 minutes in length, rather than one long one. In our classroom we may hold as many as three meetings a day, with the third at the close of the school day. Because some children arrive later or leave before the end of the day, this ensures that all children participate.

Meetings seem to work well around lunchtime. It is a time when morning energy starts to dissipate and children's concentration begins to flag. Holding a class meeting provides a change of pace. Because many problems occur during lunchtime, class meetings can be effective also just after lunch.

Sign-up

A sign-up system helps with organization, so it is clear to children wishing to discuss problems in class meetings in what order their problems will be addressed. Teachers develop various sign-up procedures. Asking preschoolers to raise their hands if they have a problem they want help resolving works well. The teacher calls on them randomly, making sure each child gets a turn. Slightly older children practicing their early literacy skills may find signing their names on a class meeting clipboard as problems arise to be very satisfying. Early primary children can use a class meeting agenda book in which they write their names and a brief description of the problem. Or the teacher may have the children themselves decide on a sign-up procedure in a meeting at the beginning of the school year.

Opening, acknowledgments, problem solving, and closing—these are the basic components of class meetings in our classroom. Teachers can adapt and use them to work for their classroom needs and their children. The next chapter describes how to introduce class meetings to the children.

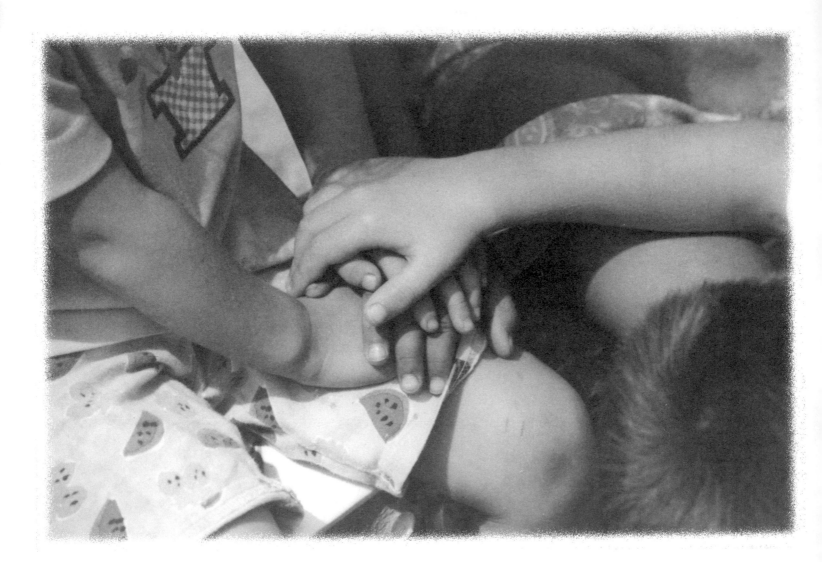

Chapter 3

Getting Started

The beginning of the school year, with its inherent excitement and stress, can be overwhelming for children of all ages— meeting new children, becoming reacquainted with familiar ones, saying goodbye to parents, anticipating new routines, becoming comfortable in a new classroom. We introduce the concept of class meetings gradually, using it first as a vehicle to bring the children together as a group and ease some of the tensions they are experiencing.

The first week we prepare the group for the meetings by talking about them when we gather for story time. We tell the children, "Next Monday we will have our first class meeting. Class meetings give us a chance to talk together, to learn how to solve problems and how to make school a safe place." To draw the children into a discussion, a teacher then says, for example, "I wonder, what does it mean for school to be a safe place?"

Setting the tone

We talk a little about what it means to make school safe. Young children tend to think of safety in physical terms. So we discuss using words rather than hitting or pushing or bullying. And then we talk about another way to feel safe—not from physical hurts, but safe from name-calling, from taunting, from being laughed at, from being excluded. I let the children know that we want school to be a place where we consider each other's feelings, where we are not afraid to speak out when something is not right, and where we listen respectfully to each other. At school we try to make others feel good about themselves.

Teachers of older children can lead similar discussions about a safe environment. Although older children may grasp the concept more quickly, they still need frequent reminders and in-depth exchanges about the importance of respectful behavior. At any age children feel safe when they can be honest with each other and with adults without fear of being reprimanded, ridiculed, punished, or treated dismissively. Class meetings serve to establish a level of trust. The teacher can explain the meetings in the context of the children becoming a close-knit, supportive, caring group in which people look out for each other's welfare—a classroom community. Activities outside class meetings also help to create a climate of cooperativeness and amicable problem solving (see "Promoting Cooperation and Problem Solving through Games," pp. 32–33).

A principal notes: "I have watched children in kindergarten through third grade participate in class discussions addressing behavior problems. Solutions to the problems or consequences are addressed, as well as acknowledgments of positive behavior. Children feel they have something to contribute. The resulting social growth may not be measurable on tests but could be far more important to the child than anything else learned in school."

Creating ground rules and guidelines

In their first meetings teachers and children can talk about treating others with respect and making the classroom a safe environment. Discussions are often somewhat chaotic and disorderly, with children speaking out of turn or creating distractions. Teachers can suggest that some ground rules are needed so people will know when they may speak and when they should listen.

Children tend to find group rules and routines more meaningful when they participate in developing them. DeVries and Kohlberg tell about a group of kindergartners who came up with the following rules for good listening:

1. Look at people when they are speaking.

2. Sit still and be silent when someone is speaking.

3. Everyone should get a chance to share.

The next day, when several children did not follow the listening ground rules, the class came up with another:

4. A person will be asked to leave the group if, after one reminder, that person continues not to follow the rules. ([1987] 1990, 159–60)

For most early childhood teachers, helping children learn to resolve conflicts with one another is a major goal. Besides class meetings, there are many ways that teachers weave conflict resolution and problem solving throughout the day and across the curriculum. Because games are interactive and highly engaging, they are excellent for fostering cooperation, problem-solving skills, and certain understandings. Here are a few cooperative games that children love to play.

Musical Shapes

Make large shapes on the floor with masking tape (two circles, two squares, two triangles). Remind children of the names and features of the shapes. Tell them that when the music stops and a shape's name is called out, everyone will try to fit inside that shape. Play music and have the children begin marching; stop the music and name a shape. Encourage and help the children to fit all their classmates into the shape. The shape should be large enough to accommodate all the children but small enough to provide a challenge.

Frozen Bean Bag

Give each child a bean bag and get some lively dancing music ready. Explain to the children that the object of the game is to help each other and to keep moving throughout the song. Show the children how to keep

Problem Solving through Games

the bean bags on their heads and bend their knees to help a friend pick up a dropped bean bag. Start the music and have the children dance around. If a bean bag slips off a child's head, he or she is frozen and needs another child's help to put it back and become unfrozen.

Do You See What I See?

In this game children explore the fact that activities and objects look different depending on the viewer's perspective or interpretation. Stand before the group and pantomime a sample activity; have the children guess the activity (for example, washing windows may look like waving to a friend or erasing the chalkboard). Invite children to act out different activities and discuss what they could be. Make the point that we all see the world differently, and the way we see the world is called our "point of view."

Musical Shapes and Frozen Bean Bag are adapted, by permission, from W. Kreidler & S.T. Whittall, *Adventures in Peacemaking: A Conflict Resolution Activity Guide for Early Childhood Educators*, 2d ed. (Cambridge, MA: Educators for Social Responsibility, and Boston: Work/Family Directions, 1999), 4–31, 4–33.
Do You See What I See? is adapted, by permission, from W.J. Kreidler, *Teaching Conflict Resolution through Children's Literature* (New York: Scholastic Professional Books, 1994), 70.

Other educators prefer to speak of *guidelines* (Gartrell 2003), *agreements* (Pirtle 1998), or *positive action statements* (Moorman 2001) rather than *rules*. Daniel Gartrell explains this difference and describes how class meetings define the "encouraging classroom":

> Guidelines—statements of "do's"—frame the standards of conduct for the encouraging classroom. In contrast, rules tend to be stated in the negative—"Don't talk when some else is." Rules tend to make teachers and children think of the classroom in terms of conformity, defiance, and enforcement. Because the intent of guidelines is to teach rather than punish, guidelines in activities like class meetings are the "gold standard" of the encouraging classroom. During the first class meetings, teachers use the creation of guidelines (through consensus whenever possible) to engender a spirit of community within the class. (personal communication 2002)

In a *Guidance Approach for the Encouraging Classroom* Gartell says,

> Class meetings, then, become a primary method for teaching democratic life skills. Each time a meeting occurs, children are reminded the classroom is a community that includes everyone, both children and adults. Just as learning centers do, class meetings help to define the encouraging classroom. (2003, 255)

Learning to give acknowledgments

The first meetings may be somewhat limited in their scope. Teachers can introduce the two key elements of a class meeting—acknowledgments and problem solving—slowly over the early weeks, or even months, of school, and they can expect young children to take a while to become active participants in the proceedings.

After opening a meeting with a group activity, the teacher can begin by modeling an acknowledgment; for example, he might say, "I would like to acknowledge Aaron for putting the scissors back where they belong this morning." He can then encourage Aaron to thank him for the acknowledgment.

Because *acknowledge* is a difficult and unfamiliar word for many preschoolers, the teacher may want to model thanking individuals as well as acknowledging them. He might say, "I would like to thank our co-teacher Sra. Naranjo for reading that story to us in Spanish" or "I would like to thank Chen and Cameron for being ready to start our meeting," and follow up by asking the class, "Do any of you have someone you would like to thank or acknowledge?"

The children may need a bit of time to think of an acknowledgment. If they still do not offer an acknowledgment, it is time to move on to a closing activity, saying, for example, "OK, then, it's time to close the meeting. Tomorrow we'll hold another class meeting. Let's try to notice good things about each other in the meantime."

Most children do not naturally remember small acts of consideration or generosity during their busy days. Recognizing and noting such acts is not an innate behavior; it is a social skill that must be learned. When we teachers observe a thoughtful gesture or act of sharing in the course of the day, we make a point of acknowledging it on the spot: "Manny, I see that you are dividing up the Goldfish crackers equally with Bernard and Jelani. Thank you for sharing the crackers fairly."

Acknowledgments begin outside class meetings—on the play-ground, in activity centers, during small-group work. Teachers model acknowledgments and encourage children to follow suit. With reminders from adults and with practice, children begin to

Recording Kind Acts

"Children, in our class we are going to watch for kind and helpful things that people do for one another. Before our meeting, I saw Nicholas help Kai find the right puzzle piece, and I wrote down Nicholas's kind act on this pad of paper in my pocket. I am sure that I will be able to write down many kind acts this morning. Then I will read them aloud in our class meeting before we go to lunch."

On the first day of school, Phyllis Whitin begins teaching her new kindergartners to show consideration, kindness, and respect and to notice when others demonstrate these qualities. She says, "Even in these first hours I want to establish the expectation that we are a community, so all the children can feel safe and respected and have their talents recognized and used by the group" (2001, 18). Whitin tries to find a kind act by every child within a few days. She is especially sure to mention the positive acts of children with potential behavior problems, to help prevent them from feeling unwanted or not valued by the group.

By the end of September, the children themselves are ready to record acts of kindness. Whitin and the children talk about ways to record: writing names, asking their friends to write their own names, drawing pictures, copying signs, and "doing the best you can" (using invented spellings). These small notes go into the Kindness Jar. Before lunch the children assemble in a circle on the rug, and the teacher opens the jar and hands the various authors their slips of paper to read to the class.

Over time the children's reports evolve. Kayla writes, "I was at the sand table. I turned around and peeked over in blocks, and Michael and Furman and Lee were playing nice." Such observations indicate that children are beginning to think beyond themselves and about the general welfare of the class. The notes acknowledging others' kindness help inspire a spirit of collaboration and mutual recognition.

By midyear kindergartners adapt the kindness notes to recognize instances of conflict resolution. Whitin writes, "Throughout the year my teacher assistant and I teach the children conflict management strategies. We review their problem-solving experiences at meeting time, and soon these events become kindness reports."

As the year goes on, the children use kindness notes to describe collaborative investigations in the science and math centers or complex games of dramatic play. They redefine kind acts to include sharing ideas and enjoying each other's company. The class has become a community.

Adapted, by permission, from P. Whitin, "Kindness in a Jar," *Young Children* 56 (September 2001): 18–22.

develop the disposition to notice and comment on others' constructive acts. (In "Recording Kind Acts," pp. 36–37, a teacher introduces a strategy to help children note one another's kindness and is pleasantly surprised by its overwhelming success in bringing the children together.)

Giving acknowledgments in class meetings reinforces this disposition. Acknowledgments make children more aware of the many opportunities to help, work with, or reach out to one another, and the positive feedback children receive makes them more likely to act on such opportunities again. What begins for children as an exercise in observation develops eventually into a climate of caring and community.

Sometimes older children who have not participated in class meetings in previous years may feel uncomfortable during the acknowledgments part of the meeting. Some may laugh or say they cannot think of anything good to say. However, as you continue to hold meetings, children learn to look forward to this part. Acknowledgments make the giver and the receiver feel good. In addition to significantly affecting the classroom climate, they build children's self-esteem. One child in our class said, "I like acknowledgments because they make me feel good inside."

When young children have not yet begun to offer contributions to the meeting, the teacher can draw them in by posing questions or using prompts: "Taylor, I noticed you and Suki playing with the soccer ball on the playground . . ." or "Alexandra, I noticed that Tanya pushed you on the swing . . ." Such statements can be followed by questions: Did you enjoy having Tanya push you on the swing? Did you go really high? Did you push Tanya on the swing?

Similarly, when young children begin to come forward with acknowledgments, engage them in brief conversations, eliciting the details of their interactions with other children. For example, if a preschool child says, "Alem, thank you for being my friend," the teacher can ask questions: What were you doing together? Did you take turns? Did you laugh? Was it fun? What makes someone a friend?

Another focus for initial class meetings is talking about and practicing I-feel statements. (See "Learning to Use I-Feel Statements," p. 40.) Learning to express negative emotions using I-feel statements begins when teachers intervene in conflicts in the classroom or on the playground. However, adopting this form of expression takes time, and teachers should model it for children whenever possible.

When most children seem to have mastered acknowledgments and I-feel statements, it is time to introduce a new element into class meetings: group problem solving.

Introducing problem solving

Just as teachers teach acknowledgments and I-feel statements in authentic situations, so they introduce the language and strategies of problem solving while helping children resolve conflicts when they occur. Mindful that she is modeling problem-solving techniques, the teacher calmly approaches a conflict between children and helps the children calm down. She listens to each child's view without expressing judgment, and validates each child's feelings. After gathering the information, the teacher restates the problem and asks the children to think of solutions that might work for them. She asks bystanders for their ideas as well.

Learning to Use I-Feel Statements

Along with acknowledgments, early class meetings can include teaching children to use I-feel statements. When the speaker uses this type of statement, she takes responsibility for her feelings rather than blaming another. For example, "You hurt me on the playground" can be restated, "I feel sad when you hurt me." Because the latter avoids accusation, the person addressed feels less threatened and may be more willing to listen. Teachers can take advantage of teachable moments during the day, when a problem arises and the accusations begin flying, to prompt children to use this phrasing.

When you intervene in a conflict, help the children involved to calm down, then encourage them to use I-feel statements: "Mitchell, use your words, not your hands. Tell Luz you feel angry when she grabs the truck you are playing with."

Role-playing is an excellent way to teach communication and social skills in class meetings. You and the children can brainstorm stressful scenarios that children their age might typically experience in the program or school setting, in the neighborhood, and at home. Then ask for volunteers to role-play these situations using I-feel statements.

When the children have mastered I-feel statements, you can extend their problem-solving skills by having them add, "Next time, will you please _____ [show some respect, be more careful, ask me if it's OK, and so on]?"

When the children with the problem decide on a solution they think can live with, they say, "Our problem is solved." In this way children become familiar with the concepts and vocabulary of problem solving before the teacher introduces it in class meetings.

Books can be an effective way to interject conflict resolution into the class meeting agenda. When a problem crops up, the teacher can select a children's book in which the characters have a similar problem and work out a solution. This technique takes planning and forethought. The teacher needs to be thoroughly familiar with the book's content (Jalongo 1986). This is especially important when books deal with feelings, attitudes, beliefs, and values.

Mary Jalongo suggests that the teacher comment on why she has chosen to read this particular book—that is, let the children know that a certain classroom incident or problem made her think about sharing the book with them—and that the teacher pose questions as she reads: "Questions that encourage children to analyze the behavior of story characters, make inferences about emotional reactions, apply information to their own experience, and synthesize techniques for coping with crises are all appropriate" (1986, 46).

Finally the teacher summarizes the story, rephrases the basic concepts, and responds to children's questions, reinforcing ideas and points relevant to the classroom conflict at issue.

Or the teacher might read a familiar story such as "Goldilocks and the Three Bears" and ask for volunteers to act it out. Role-playing can help children better understand a storybook character's motives and feelings. By switching roles, children can be encouraged to see a problem from more than one point of view (Wittmer & Honig 1994). Through role play children can begin to grasp social skills like empathy and perspective taking that are crucial to problem solving. At the end of the chapter, we include "Children's Books for Building Conflict Resolution Skills" (pp. 44–45), a brief annotated list of books that lend themselves to children's group discussions about problem solving. (See also "Select Bibliography," pp. 76–79, for more children's books in [Spanish as well as English] and books for young adults, teachers, and parents.)

When the teacher introduces the first classroom problems to be resolved in class meeting, she should do so in general terms without mentioning names: "Yesterday at the water table there was some arguing and grabbing, and a lot of water spilled on the floor and on people's shoes and socks. I wonder what we can do so that this problem does not occur again at the water table. Does anyone have an idea?" The teacher then guides discussion, prompting the children by modeling the use of the problem-solving language they use to determine solutions to individual conflicts. With a problem posed this way, children are less likely to feel defensive, and the issue becomes a general one requiring everyones's involvement (Kriedler & Whittall 1999.)

After the children tackle a few such disputes, and when the teacher senses that they are ready, she can begin to have children introduce individual conflicts in class meeting. On the playground she might say, "Bart, I see that you and Renee are having trouble taking turns on the red trike. I've noticed other people having the same problem. That is a very popular tricycle. Would you and Renee agree to explain your problem in class meeting today? Perhaps the entire class can do some thinking and come up with ways to share the trike." Teachers will be amazed at how willingly children set aside their disagreements and get on with the business of playing and learning when they know the problem will be cleared up later in class meeting.

Glasser says,

> If children learn to participate in a problem-solving group when they enter school and continue to do so with a variety of teachers throughout the six years of elementary school, they learn that the world is not a mysterious and sometimes hostile and frightening place where they have little control over what happens to them. They learn that, although the world may be difficult and that it may at times appear hostile and mysterious, they can use their brains individually and as a group to solve the problems of living in their school world. (1969, 123)

Such benefits can begin, we find, even in preschool and kindergarten. We have looked closely at acknowledgments and problem solving, the key elements of our class meetings, and described how we introduce them to children in the beginning of the year. Now we turn to several ways that meetings can be varied or adapted.

Children's Books for Building Conflict Resolution Skills

Bourgeois, Paulette. *Franklin Is Bossy*. **New York: Scholastic, 1993.** Franklin learns about the give-and-take inherent in friendship. Useful for discussing the importance of talking about feelings.

Bruchac, Joseph. *The First Strawberries: A Cherokee Story*. **New York: Dial, 1993.** A traditional tale about how the wonder of strawberries helps a wife and husband settle their conflict. Useful for discussing adult conflicts.

Clifton, Lucille. *Three Wishes*. **New York: Viking, 1976.** A magic penny leads to a conflict and solution between two best friends. Useful for discussing lose-lose solutions, how conflicts escalate, and conflicts with friends.

DePaola, Tomie. *The Knight and the Dragon*. **New York: Putnam, 1990.** The knight and the dragon prepare to fight until the royal librarian comes up with a better idea. Good for talking about finding peaceful solutions.

Graham, Bob. *This is Our House*. **Cambridge, MA: Candlewick, 1996.** George says only he can use the large cardboard carton house and refuses to let other children play in it. But they have other ideas. Good for working on prejudices and antibias, conflicts over playmates, and sharing play materials.

Greenfield, Eloise. *First Pink Light*. **New York: Black Butterfly, 1976.** Mother and son negotiate a conflict in this poignant story about waiting for the father to come home.

Guback, Georgia. *Luka's Quilt*. **New York: Greenwillow, 1994.** Luka and her grandmother have a conflict over how the quilt her grandmother is making for her should look. They come up with a solution that satisfies them both. Excellent for discussing win-win solutions.

Havill, Juanita. *Jamaica and Brianna*. **Boston: Houghton Mifflin, 1993.** Two friends make hurtful comments about each other's boots until they realize that what they say hurts. Good for discussions about different points of view and put-downs.

Havill, Juanita. *Jamaica Tag-Along*. **Boston: Houghton Mifflin, 1989.** Jamaica is distressed that her older brother won't let her play. Another child messes up her sand castle. In the end the three children find a way to work together. Excellent for discussing different points of view, how one's actions affect others, and conflicts among siblings.

Hoffman, Mary. *Amazing Grace.* **New York: Dial, 1991.** Grace wants to play the role of Peter Pan in the school play. Another child tells her she can't be Peter Pan because she is Black. But she can play the role, and she does! A good book to talk about problem solving and counteracting bias statements.

Jones, Rebecca C. *Matthew and Tilly.* **New York: Dutton, 1991.** Matthew and Tilly are best friends until Matthew breaks Tilly's purple crayon. A good story for working on conflicts between friends, escalation, and different kinds of solutions to conflict.

Lionni, Leo. *Six Crows.* **New York: Scholastic, 1988.** The farmer and the crows fight over the same wheat fields until they learn the value of communication. Good for focusing on communicating feelings and needs.

Lionni, Leo. *Swimmy.* **New York: Scholastic, 1963.** A small fish organizes the other fish to stand up to the big fish. Can be used to talk about many aspects of conflict resolution.

Marsden, Carolyn. The Gold-Threaded Dress. Cambridge, MA: Candlewick, 2002. A young Thai American girl takes her ceremonial Thai dance dress to school, where her classmates insist on trying it on. Disaster results. Good book for discussions about peer pressure, bullying, and cultural awareness.

Scieszka, Jon. *The True Story of the Three Little Pigs by A. Wolf.* **New York: Scholastic, 1989.** The popular fairy tale told from the point of view of the Big Bad Wolf. Excellent for working on perspective taking.

Seuss, Dr. *The Sneeches and Other Stories.* **New York: Random House, 1961.** Three good stories about conflict. "The Sneeches" is especially good for talking about antibias issues. "The Zax" is good for talking about lose-lose solutions to conflicts.

Silverman, Erica. *Don't Fidget a Feather.* **New York: Macmillan, 1994.** Duck and Gander always compete over who's best. One day their contest leads to big trouble, until one of them decides not to compete. Excellent for discussing win-lose, lose-lose, and win-win solutions, as well as competitive (winner-loser) games.

Zolotow, Charlotte. *The Hating Book.* **New York: Harper Trophy, 1969.** A little girl learns the value of communication and preserves her friendship with her best friend. Good for focusing on relationships and communication skills.

Adapted, by permission, from N. Carlsson-Paige & D.E. Levin, *Before Push Comes to Shove: Building Conflict Resolution Skills with Children* (St. Paul, MN: Redleaf, 1998), 87–89.

Chapter 4

Variations

In this chapter we look at several types of class meetings and problem-solving contexts that vary in one way or another from the basic class meeting. The first is the bilingual meeting, in which the teacher and children conduct the meeting using both English and Spanish (or another language). Next we consider occasions when problem solving takes place with only the children directly involved in an incident or problem rather than with the whole class. Included here is Lisa Clifford's description of negotiation chairs and problem solving with young children.

Finally, Sylvia Chard discusses the uses of class meetings in the project approach. While these group meetings differ from the meetings described earlier, with their focus on solving children's interpersonal problems, Chard's discussion shows how in collaborative work children's problem solving and thinking together strengthen the skills used in class meetings and vice versa.

Bilingual class meetings

A teacher observed: "Children who are monolingual English or Spanish speakers want to quickly learn the words [in the second language] to acknowledge or voice a concern. Class meetings provide a support system for dual language use in our classroom and the opportunity for children to volunteer as translators or mediators—educational and empowering roles for children."

Bilingual class meetings provide a comfortable, meaningful environment in which children can use both their first and second languages. Through bilingual class meetings children are quick to learn highly used, patterned responses in a second language, such as "I would like to acknowledge Lupita" or "*Quiero dar un reconocimiento a Lupita.*"

In our classroom we alternate the language we use in the opening acknowledgments and problem-solving questions. Children sometimes speak in their first language and ask the help of a peer in translating. Often, however, a child speaks in the language of the other person involved in the problem, even when it is not her primary language. The strong desire to communicate her feelings to the other child motivates the speaker to make the extra effort.

If both children speak the same first language, it is easy for them to begin talking to each other. In this case, it is helpful to give an occasional update to the children who are not fluent in the language the children are using. Appointing other children to translate is an ideal way to involve more children in the meeting.

A bilingual class meeting usually takes longer, but the benefits for primary and secondary language acquisition are tremendous. The important point is that children are more likely to learn a language when they are highly motivated to use it. When two children have a problem, the need to communicate their feelings to one another is powerful.

In one bilingual meeting Elizabeth, a child who speaks only English, sought to solve a name-calling problem with Selena, a Spanish speaker. On this particular day the meeting was being facilitated in Spanish. Elizabeth needed a classmate to help translate so all the children could understand. Alberto said he would do this. Sometimes the teacher can ask more than one child to help with translating in order to actively engage more children in the meeting.

Maestra [Teacher]: *¿Quién quiere solucionar algún problema?*

Elizabeth: *(raising her hand)* I have a problem. Selena calls me names on the playground.

Alberto: *(telling Selena what Elizabeth just said) Elizabeth dice que tú le pones sobrenombres.*

Selena: *Mentirosa.*

Alberto: *(to Elizabeth)* She says you are lying.

Elizabeth: No, I'm not lying. You know you called me names and I don't like it.

Alberto: *(to Selena) Dice que ella no está mintiendo. Que tú le pusiste sobrenombres y eso no le gusta.*

Selena says nothing.

Maestra: ¿Selena, recuerdas si eso ocurrió? [Selena, do you remember that this happened?]

Selena: *Sí.* [Yes.]

Maestra: Gracias por ser sincera, Selena. Me complace que estés dispuesta a resolver este problema. Gracias. [Thank you for being honest, Selena. I'm glad you're ready to solve this problem. Thank you.] *¿Elizabeth, tienes alguna solución?*

Alberto: Elizabeth, do you have a solution?

Elizabeth: Yes. I want to shake hands.

Common Spanish Phrases Used in Class Meetings

Quiero hacer un reconocimiento _____. [I want to acknowledge _____.]

Quiero hacerle un reconocimiento a _____. [I want to give an acknowledgment to _____.]

Reconocimiento [Acknowledgment]

¿Quién quiere resolver un problema? [Who wants to solve a problem?]

Gracias por ser sincera. [Thank you for being honest.]

¿Tienes alguna solución? [Do you have a solution?]

Quiero que nos demos la mano. [I want to shake hands.]

Quiero darte un abrazo. [I want to give you a hug.]

Quiero pedir perdón. [or] *Quiero decir que lo siento.* [I want to say sorry.]

Mi problema está resuelto. [My problem is solved.]

¿Qué aprendiste hoy? [What did you learn today?]

¿Quién quiere traducir? [Who wants to translate?]

¿Quién quiere hacer un reconocimiento? [Who wants to give an acknowledgment?]

¿Quieres tratar de resolver este problema? [Do you want to try to solve this problem?]

¿Alguien más tiene algún problema? [Does anyone else have a problem?]

Alberto: *Selena, Elizabeth quiere darte la mano.*

Maestra: *¿Selena, estás dispuesta a hacerlo?* [Selena, are you ready to   do that?]

Selena: *Si.* [Yes.]

The two girls go to the center of the circle and shake hands.

Maestra: *¿Qué aprendiste hoy?* [What did you learn today?]

Selena: *No voy a poner más sobrenombres.*

Alberto: She is not going to call names.

Elizabeth: *Gracias.* [Thank you.]

Maestra: *¿Se resolvió tu problema?* [Is your problem solved?]

Elizabeth: My problem is solved. How do I say it in Spanish? *Mi problema está resuelto.*

Young children tend to become confused if the translator speaks in the first person ("I want to shake hands"), as if he himself were the involved party. It seems to be less confusing when the translating child uses the third person: "Selena, Elizabeth wants to shake hands."

Solving problems in small groups

Not every topic is appropriate for community meeting. Some issues are likely to cause children embarrassment. Others need to be dealt with right when they occur. For any of several reasons, the teacher may decide that in a given instance a class meeting is not the way to go. In such cases, as in larger class meetings, it is important for the children themselves to take ownership of the problem-solving process (McClurg 1998).

Mini meetings

It may be the child's personality or the nature of the problem, or both, that makes a smaller meeting preferable in a particular instance. Yvette, for example, is a quiet child who is more comfortable talking in small groups than in whole-class meetings. Consequently, during class meetings she seldom speaks out if she has a problem.

One day Yvette told me she had a problem she with three girls who were ignoring her during lunch. I thanked her for taking the initiative to solve the problem. I asked her if she wanted to discuss

this issue during a class meeting. She opted instead for a private meeting with the three girls, and in the meeting they successfully resolved the issue.

Yvette continued using mini meetings as a method of addressing problems. Although she never discussed a problem in a large class meeting, she began talking more to the teachers because of her growing confidence and sense of trust from the success of the mini meeting alternative.

Some teachers may be reluctant to use class meetings, fearing that an issue will unexpectedly be introduced that embarrasses a child or is inappropriate for group discussion. But in fact the teacher can quickly step in if such a problem arises. Certainly sensitive issues do come up in class meetings from time to time—issues related to sexual conduct, personal hygiene, or racism, for example. Or a child from an abusive home may bring up matters that require the attention of the school counselor or a decision about notifying social services or the authorities.

If such a topic is broached in a class meeting, the teacher can tactfully head off discussion and opt to address the subject with the child in private or suggest that the children involved meet later with her in a mini meeting. What is important is children's learning that all problems can be addressed; nothing has to remain secret or hidden.

Negotiation chairs

For problem solving, negotiation chairs in the preschool classroom are a wonderful addition to class meeting. When two young children have an interpersonal problem that can't wait until class meeting, they sit in negotiation chairs to discuss it and decide on a solution. Any two chairs can serve as the negotiation chairs, or you can designate two special chairs.

My method of introducing the negotiation chairs is simple and straightforward. Having decided on a prearranged problem and solution, Brian the teacher aide and I role-play the problem during free choice activities. Brian grabs a crayon from me and I snatch it back, saying, "You can't take my crayon." Brian responds, "I was using it first." I say, "No, you weren't; I was. We have a problem."

By this time our voices are loud and angry. Many of the children stop their free choice activities to listen.

Brian asks, "How can we solve our problem?" I suggest, "Let's use our words and talk about our problem." Brian agrees.

I point to two chairs: "Let's sit in these chairs and talk. We'll negotiate—that means work out our problem together. We can call them negotiation chairs." As we sit down, I say, "I'm so mad because you took away my crayon. You didn't ask me first." Brian says, "I was using it before you were."

Lisa Clifford, who wrote and contributed the "Negotiation Chairs" portion of this chapter (pp. 53–55), taught preschool at Pueblo Garden Elementary School in Tucson, Arizona.

Variations

The children are very curious and are now seated on the floor in front of us. At this point I invite the entire class to help us with ideas for solving the crayon problem: "Does anyone have an idea how Brian and I can solve this problem?" We give the children time to think and to tell their ideas.

Rob says, "Say sorry." Lulu says, "Don't fight." Antonia says, "Use kind words." Imani says, "Have Brian ask you for the crayon before he uses it."

The person with the problem selects the solution that feels right. I decide to use Imani's idea—have Brian ask me if he can use the crayon instead of just taking it. I ask Brian if he agrees to this solution, and he says yes. I look at him and say, "Our problem is solved." Brian affirms this by repeating "Our problem is solved."

On another day Jack brought a toy turtle to school. Sam took it from him. Jack came over to tell me about the problem. By the time we had worked through the problem using the negotiation chairs, Jack was smiling and Sam had his arm around him. Sam said, "I'm going to use the turtle for a little while, then Jack is going to use it after me."

Using negotiation chairs is not a technique preschoolers can master after one demonstration. It is important for adults to continue modeling the use of negotiation chairs as often as possible to resolve a variety of problems throughout the school year.

When a child refuses to use the negotiation chairs, I say, "I can see you are not ready to solve the problem. We don't have to solve all our problems. If you change your mind, you can still use the negotiation chairs."

Negotiation chairs are a good prelude or complement to class meetings. There are always situations where waiting for a class meeting is not advisable. When such a conflict arises, negotiation chairs are quick and effective.

Class meetings in the project approach

Many teachers regularly offer opportunities for children to make choices and take ownership of tasks. Class meetings can help all children attain developmentally appropriate levels of achievement in individualized work and provide a forum for collaborative planning as well. During class meetings, teachers can present task alternatives and help children make appropriate choices.

The project approach is one framework that works especially well with class meetings. As described in *Engaging Children's Minds: The Project Approach* (Katz & Chard 2001), projects are in-depth studies of topics or themes such as bicycles, birds, or the desert, and the project approach enables children to make choices and work independently while exploring those studies. During project work, children choose from among alternatives, develop individual interests, and undertake independent investigations responsibly. Children can also develop strategies for solving problems on their own or with friends, and many projects are collaborative studies in which all children in the class take part.

Project work is a beneficial but challenging teaching strategy, and class meetings can address these challenges through increased communication. When teachers share the planning of project work with the class, children feel ownership in the way projects develop. Throughout the study, class meetings can be used as a venue for children to share plans, interesting features of their work, and ideas for new directions.

Sylvia C. Chard, Ph.D., a leading expert on the project approach, wrote and contributed the section titled "Class Meetings in the Project Approach" (pp. 56–60) in this chapter. Sylvia is an associate professor in the Department of Elementary Education at the University of Alberta in Edmonton.

As they learn to appreciate the work of their classmates, children are better able to evaluate their own efforts as well. Finally, children can celebrate the conclusion of a project by using class meetings to plan a culminating event before moving on to a new study.

Planning project work and getting started. Class meetings are an excellent time to introduce a topic of study. During the first phase of the project (about a week in duration), the class can discuss relevant personal experiences and reflect on what they already know about the

---

Components of a Project-Oriented Class Meeting

When doing project work during class meetings, the following components are particularly helpful:

• **Sharing** (telling others about what you are doing, listening to what others tell you about what they are doing) interests, expertise, achievements, concerns, intentions

• **Problem solving** (recognizing when there is a problem that can be solved appropriately by class meetings), problem stating, seeking solutions

• **Acknowledging** (appreciating individual children who have facilitated other children's work) help given, ideas, practical help obtaining material, appreciation by other children

• **Modeling** (the appropriate, the optimum) dispositions that support learning by helping children solve problems independently, seek advice from other children and/or the teacher, become deeply involved in work, concentrate, and be persistent

---

topic. Teachers and children can brainstorm questions they would like to investigate and ways of documenting their experience and knowledge, such as drawing and dramatic play.

Developing projects. The second phase of project work involves fieldwork, conducted either in the classroom through the study of real objects and interviewing experts or by taking the children outside the classroom walls to a local field site. During class meetings, children can share what they have learned from these investigations and remind one another of the various ways of representing what they are learning about the topic.

Once the project is well under way, children often pursue their own individual interests; class meetings enable children to share their unique interests and questions while demonstrating the particular contribution their work is making to the collaborative study as a whole.

Evaluation and modeling. Class meetings provide teachers with an opportunity to point out the most valuable features of children's work. Sometimes a teacher will comment on original or imaginative ideas in a child's work, while in other instances it will be the care and attention to detail or a neat and attractive presentation that is pointed out. Particular strengths of children's work can be emphasized for the benefit of the class. Children will often strive to improve their work and be more confident in their efforts when they have appropriate models.

Concluding projects. In class meetings children can plan an event at the end of the project for sharing their work with others, including parents, grandparents, and other children. Through collaborative

Ten Essential Questions in Project Work

In a class project a few essential questions regularly arise. Class meetings provide a good opportunity for the group to discuss these questions.

1. What aspects of the topic shall we study? [¿Qué aspectos del tema debemos estudiar?]

2. What experience do we have of the topic? [¿Qué experiencia tenemos en este tema?]

3. What questions do we have about the topic? [¿Qué preguntas tenemos sobre este tema?]

4. Who might know some of the answers? [¿Quién puede saber algunas de las respuestas?]

5. Where can we go to find out? [¿A dónde podemos dirigirnos para encontrar respuestas ?]

6. Which books can help us? [¿Qué libros nos puede servir?]

7. What are we each most interested in? [¿Qué es lo que más le interesa a cada uno?]

8. How can we represent what we are learning? [¿Cómo podemos representar lo que estamos aprendiendo?]

9. What are the highlights of the project when it is completed? [¿Qué se destacará del proyecto cuando esté terminado?]

10. How can we share what we have learned with others? [¿Cómo podemos compartir lo que hayamos aprendido con otros?]

All of these questions are of importance to both teachers and children, although teachers may have more expertise in answering some of them. These questions will help teachers and children become more familiar with project work, enabling rich discussions that lead to a greater understanding of the topic at hand. In turn, children will learn to take initiative in their work and to be accountable to the class for their individual contributions to the project.

evaluation the children will decide the most important parts of the study to be shared, and how to do so. Perhaps they will perform a skit about an expert they interviewed or show a series of pictures explaining a process they have used. These kinds of decisions are useful in involving children in reflection and evaluation of the project as a whole.

As the project proceeds. In addition to the questions that come up regularly during project work (see "Ten Essential Questions in Project Work," p. 59), others arising throughout the life of a project can be addressed in class meetings, such as What stories and knowledge do we or our families have to share about our experiences of the topic? Which tasks or activities can we accomplish? What are some of the most interesting fieldwork observations? What are some ways of representing what we've learned? Who will come to share the learning of the class at the end of the study? How will they be invited? Who will write letters of thanks to guests who have helped in the study?

As children address questions like these, they develop a shared understanding of the process of studying a topic in depth. Reflections and discussions during class meetings help children appreciate their learning community and realize that they have made a personal contribution to a corporate effort. They are gaining important skills— not only for the classroom, but also for learning effectively throughout their lives.

The variations are endless

We have examined several variations on the basic class meeting theme: bilingual meetings, meeting in small groups, using negotiation chairs, and working on group projects in class meetings. Other variations will evolve as individual teachers develop meeting procedures and other problem-solving formats that work best for them and the children in their classes. As in all our teaching, we plan carefully, and then we learn as we go along. The children themselves are always teaching us.

Frequently Asked
Questions
. . . and the Facts

When we talk with other teachers and parents about class meetings, here are some of the questions that often arise and, in a nutshell, our responses.

Don't class meetings take valuable time away from teaching?

IN FACT: *Class meetings not only save time by reducing discipline problems but also accomplish other cognitive and social-emotional goals for children.*

Rather than wasting learning time, the meetings actually save time that would be taken up with discipline problems and interpersonal conflicts. In many instances, problems that would otherwise interrupt children's learning can be tabled until meeting time. Once children are used to solving conflicts in class meetings, they tend to wait and bring up problems at the meeting rather than demand the teacher's immediate attention during classroom activities. This frees up the rest of the day to focus on learning.

Knowing their problems will be addressed improves children's ability to concentrate. Further, when children master the problem-solving strategies used in class meetings, they use these strategies to solve problems on their own. The problem solving and perspective taking that occur in group meetings strengthen children's use of such skills in other areas of the curriculum.

When a conflict arises, I usually try to help the children involved to resolve it right then and there. Do class meetings have any value *beyond* the benefits of the on-the-spot problem solving?

IN FACT: *While on-the-spot problem solving with children has an important place, there are times when addressing problems in class meetings is preferable and times when doing both is worthwhile.*

Extended conflict resolution right after a problem erupts may or may not be a good idea in a particular instance. The children may be too upset to think clearly. There's also the time that is spent and the likelihood that children's engagement in learning is interrupted. Having the option of class meetings allows for tabling a problem that is likely to take some real working through. Since the children themselves sign up for a meeting, they take responsibility for resolving their problem. Another added benefit of the class meeting is that brain-

Another principal says: "I can see differences in children from classrooms that hold class meetings and children from classrooms using methods that deal only with behavior control. Children from classrooms with class meetings are empowered to use a number of alternatives when resolving conflicts, and they tend to take more responsibility for their actions. They also seem to have an investment in each other and work as a more cohesive group."

storming and evaluating possible solutions as a group tend to produce a wider range of ideas and more thoughtful consideration of what might work. Children often see problems more clearly when they themselves are not directly involved. We all do, in fact. By listening to two or more perspectives on a problem—someone else's problem—the children who are not involved in the original episode learn that a situation can look quite different depending on one's point of view.

Doesn't the teacher risk losing control of the classroom when he shares authority with the children?

IN FACT: *In expressing their opinions in class meeting, children may sometimes become emotional and discussion heated, but the results are positive.*

Some teachers who want to maintain their position of authority in the classroom may object to giving children any control. They are afraid that group problem solving will result in chaos. But in a well-run class meeting, the teacher guides discussion and helps children stay on track. If teachers follow the basic guidelines presented in this book, class meetings are orderly and effective. Rather than detract from effective classroom management, the meetings contribute to it.

I worry about sensitive issues coming up in the group situation.

IN FACT: *The teacher facilitates group meetings, so she can quickly step in if a problem seems likely to cause a child embarrassment or be inappropriate for class discussion.*

Sensitive issues do come up in meetings from time to time—sexual conduct, personal hygiene, or racism, for example. When a child makes a negative remark about someone else's race, gender, or disability, the teacher can often engage the children in an antibias conversation right then (for guidance, see Derman-Sparks and the A.B.C. Task Force 1989; Levin 1994 [Chapter 6]). Alternatively, the teacher may choose to handle a biased remark in a matter-of-fact way and then engage the children in a fuller discussion later.

Children from abusive homes may bring up matters that require the attention of the school counselor or a decision about notifying social services or the authorities. When this happens, the teacher can head off discussion and address the subject with the child in private or suggest that the children involved meet later with her in

a mini meeting. The important point is that children learn that all problems can be addressed; nothing has to remain secret or hidden.

What should I do when the children come up with a solution that seems very unlikely to work?

IN FACT: *The teacher helps the children to arrive at a workable solution and also to recognize that sometimes a solution has to be changed or another one tried.*

During the meeting teachers can pose questions to help the children evaluate an idea and to consider different scenarios ("What if someone takes a really long turn and other people get tired of waiting?"). The challenge in thinking ahead like this is itself beneficial, and it often helps improve the solution the children work out. Not every idea has to work out beautifully. The children learn something important when the first solution they decide on does not work and they have to modify or replace it—either on the spot or later in a class meeting.

Aren't bilingual class meetings cumbersome and confusing for young children?

IN FACT: *Problem-solving interaction in a bilingual meeting is an excellent way for children to learn a second language.*

Children in bilingual classrooms quickly become familiar with commonly used phrases in both their first and second languages during class meetings. Acquiring the phrases and vocabulary of problem solving in a second language has real value and meaning to children; they realize it allows them to express their feelings directly to the other child involved in a conflict. They begin to learn the other language through purposeful use, not by memorizing words without a meaningful context. Refer back to Chapter 4 (pp. 48–51) for information on how to conduct the bilingual class meeting effectively.

Classroom Charts

Teachers, you can copy these prompts (pp. 69–73) on poster board and hang them in the classroom for easy reference.

Class Meeting

1. opening
2. acknowledgments
3. problem solving
4. closing

Reunión del grupo

1. inicio
2. reconocimientos
3. cómo solucionar problemas
4. cierre

© Copyright 1995 Patricia Jiménez Weaver. Translation adapted by permission.

Problem-Solving Strategies for Interpersonal Conflicts

Talk to the other person.
Ignore the other person.
Move away.
Ask someone for help.
Act it out.

© Copyright 1995 Patricia Jiménez Weaver and Emily Vance.

Premeeting Problem-Solving Steps

1. Calm down; take some deep breaths.

2. Talk to the person with whom you are having a problem. Use "I-feel" statements.

I feel _____ when you _____ because _____.
      (feeling)   *(problem behavior)*   *(how the behavior affects me)*

Next time I would like you to _____.
                               (preferable behavior)

The other person involved in the problem repeats:

Next time I will _____
             (preferable behavior)

3. Move away from the person involved in the problem.

4. If the problem continues, sign up for class meeting.

Pasos para solucionar problemas antes de las reuniones

1. Tranquilízate y respira profundo varias veces.

2. Habla con quien tengas algún problema. Usa afirmaciones acompañadas de "Yo me siente . . . ."

Yo me siento _____ cuando tú _____porque _____.
      (sentimiento)   *(comportamiento problemático)*   *(cómo me afecta el comportamiento)*

La próxima vez me gustaría que tú _____.
                              (comportamiento preferible)

La persona involucrada en el problema repite:

La próxima vez yo_____.
                     (repite el comportamiento preferible)

3. Aléjate de la persona involucrada en el problema.

4. Si el problema continúa, anota tu nombre en la lista para tener una reunión del grupo.

Words to Describe Feelings

Anger/Hostility

Mad
Angry
Furious
Bitter
Envious
Disgusted
Cheated
Upset

Frustration

Frustrated
Exasperated

Fear/Anxiety

Frightened
Anxious
Threatened
Scared
Worried
Nervous

Positive Feelings

Happy	Amused
Delighted	Pleased
Cheerful	Grateful
Surprised	Hopeful
Enthusiastic	Glad
Excited	

High Self-Esteem

Competent	Secure
Confident	Important
Determined	Appreciated
Proud	
Capable	
Needed	

Support

Caring
Loving
Sympathy
Pity

Negative Feelings

Embarrassed	Unimportant
Ashamed	Regretful
Humiliated	Unsure
Guilty	Intimidated
Insecure	Uncertain
Neglected	Left out
Doubtful	Unappreciated

Palabras que describen los sentimientos

Coraje/Hostalidad

enfadado/a
enfurecido/a
furioso/a
amargado/a
envidioso/a
asqueado/a
traicionado/a
molesto/a

Frustración

frustrado/a
exasperado/a

Temor/Ansiedad

asustado/a
ansioso/a
amenazado/a
atemorizado/a
preocupado/a
nervioso/a

Setimientos positivos

alegre, feliz
encantado/a
contento/a
sorprendido/a
entusiasmado/a
emocionado/a

entretenido/a
complacido/a
agradecido/a
esperanzado/a

Gran autoestima

competente
confiado/a
decidido/a
orgulloso/a
capaz
necesitado/a

seguro/a
importante
apreciado/a

Sentimientos ngativos

turbado/a

avergonzado/a

humillado/a

culpable

inseguro/a

ignorado/a

dudoso/a

sin importancia

arrepentido/a

inseguro/a

intimidado/a

indeciso/a

excluido/a

despreciado/a

Respaldo

cuidadoso/a

cariñoso/a

simpático/a

compasivo/a

References

Brophy, J.E. 1981. Teacher praise: A functional analysis. *Review of Educational Research* 51 (1): 5–32.

Carlsson-Paige, N., & D.E. Levin. 1998. *When push comes to shove: Building conflict resolution skills with children.* St. Paul, MN: Redleaf.

Day, C.B. 2000. Foreword. In *That's not fair! A teacher's guide to activism with young children,* eds. A. Pelo & F. Davidson, x. St. Paul, MN: Redleaf.

Derman-Sparks, L., & the A.B.C. Task Force. 1989. *Anti-bias curriculum: Tools for empowering young children.* Washington, DC: NAEYC.

DeVries, R., & L. Kohlberg. [1987] 1990. *Constructivist early education: Overview and comparison with other programs.* Washington, DC: NAEYC.

Dinwiddie, S.A. 1994. The saga of Sally, Sammy, and the red pen: Facilitating children's social problem solving. *Young Children* 49 (5): 13–19.

Gartrell, D. 2003. *A guidance approach for the encouraging classroom.* Albany, NY: Delmar/Thomson Learning.

Glasser, W. 1969. *Schools without failure.* New York: Harper & Row.

Harris, T.T., & J.D. Fuqua. 2000. What goes around comes around: Building a community of learners through circle times. *Young Children* 55 (1): 44–47.

Helm, J.H., & L.G. Katz. 2001. *Young investigators: The project approach in the early years.* New York: Teachers College Press, and Washington, DC: NAEYC.

Jalongo, M.R. 1986. Using crisis-oriented books with young children. In *Reducing stress in young children's lives,* ed. J.B. McCracken, 41–46. Washington, DC: NAEYC.

Katz, L., & S. Chard. 2001. *Engaging children's minds: The project approach.* Greenwich, CT: Ablex.

Kohn, Alfie. 1999. *Punished by rewards: The trouble with gold stars, incentive plans, A's, praise, and other bribes.* New York: Houghton-Mifflin.

Kreidler, W.J. 1994. *Teaching conflict resolution through children's literature.* New York: Scholastic Professional Books.

Kreidler, W.J., & S.T. Whittall. 1999. *Early childhood adventures in peacemaking: A conflict resolution guide for early childhood educators.* 2d ed. Cambridge, MA: Educators for Social Responsibility, and Boston: Work/Family Directions.

Levin, D. 1994. *Teaching young children in violent times.* Cambridge, MA: Educators for Social Responsiblilty.

Logan, T. 1998. Creating a kindergarten community. *Young Children* 53 (2): 22–26.

McClurg, L.G. 1998. Building an ethical community in the classroom: Community meeting. *Young Children* 53 (2): 30–35.

Moorman, C. 2001. *Spirit whisperers: Teachers who nourish a child's spirit.* Merrill, MI: Personal Power.

Pelo, A., & F. Davidson. 2000. *That's not fair! A teacher's guide to activism with young children.* St. Paul, MN: Redleaf.

Pirtle, S. 1998. *Linking up!* Cambridge, MA: Educators for Social Responsibility.

Stipek, D.J. 1998. Reinforcement theory. *Motivation to learn,* 19–38. New York: Viacom.

Styles, D. 2001. *Class meetings: Building leadership, problem-solving, and decision-making skills in the respectful classroom.* Markham, Ontario: Pembroke. (Distributed in the U.S. by Stenhouse).

Whitin, P. 2001. Kindness in a jar. *Young Children* 56 (5): 18–22.

Wittmer, D.S., & A.S. Honig. 1994. Encouraging positive social development in young children. *Young Children* 49 (5): 4–12.

Select Bibliography

Children's Books

Alder, Katie, & Rachael McBride. *For Sale: One Sister—Cheap*. Danbury, CT: Children's Press, 1986. (Frustration)

Alexander, Martha. *Even That Moose Won't Listen to Me*. New York: Dial Books for Young Readers, 1988. (Problem solving)

Bang, Molly. *Wiley and the Hairy Man*. New York: Aladdin, 1996. (Bullying)

Begaye, Lisa Shook. *Building a Bridge*. Flagstaff, AZ: Northland, 1993. (Friendship)

Birdseye, Tom. *Airmail to the Moon*. New York: Holiday House, 1989. (Feelings)

Carle, Eric. *The Mixed-Up Chameleon*. New York: Crowell, 1984. (Self-esteem)

Carlson, Nancy. *I Like Me*. Parsippany, NJ: Pearson Education, 1990. (Identity)

Hoffman, Mary. *Amazing Grace*. Glenview, IL: Scott Foresman, 1991. (Self-esteem)

Joseph, Lynn. *Jasmine's Parlour Day*. New York: Lothrop, Lee & Shepard, 1994. (Sharing)

Knight, Margy Burns. *Who Belongs Here? An American Story.* Gardiner, ME: Tilbury House, 1993. (Prejudice)

Marsden, Carolyn. *The Gold-Threaded Dress.* Cambridge, MA: Candlewick, 2002. (Diversity)

Mitchell, Margaree King. *Uncle Jed's Barbershop.* New York: Aladdin, 1998. (Perseverance, courage)

Moss, Thylias. *I Want To Be.* New York: Puffin, 1998. (Self-esteem)

Osofsky, Audrey. *My Buddy.* New York: Henry Holt, 1994. (Friendship, disability)

Prestine, Joan Singleton. *Sometimes I Feel Awful* (Kids Have Feelings, Too, Series). Carthage, IL: Fearon Teacher Aids, 1993. (Feelings)

Rayner, Mary. *Garth Pig Steals the Show.* New York: Dutton, 1993. (Problem solving)

Silverstein, Shel. *The Giving Tree.* New York: HarperCollins, 1986. (Selfishness, giving, friendship)

Simon, Norma. *Nobody's Perfect, Not Even My Mother.* Morton Grove, IL: Albert Whitman, 1987. (Success)

Talley, Carol. *Clarissa.* Kansas City, MO: Marsh Media, 1992. (Problem solving)

Udry, Janice May. *Let's Be Enemies.* New York: Scholastic, 1961. (Friendship)

Walter, Mildred Pitts. *Two and Too Much.* New York: Simon & Schuster, 1990. (Responsibility)

Children's Books in Spanish

Ada, Alma Flor. *Amigos* (Friends). Miami, FL: Santillana, 1999. *(Auto-estima)*

Ada, Alma Flor. *No era yo* (It wasn't me). Miami, FL: Santillana, 2000. *(Responsabilidad)*

Ada, Alma Flor. *La jaula dorada* (The golden cage). Miami, FL: Santillana, 2000. *(Sensibilidad)*

Alba, Juanita. *Calor, A Story of Warmth for All Ages.* New York: Lectorum, 1996. *(Sentimientos, amor)*

Covault, Ruth M. *Pablo y Pimienta* (Pablo and Pimienta). Flagstaff, AZ: Northland, 1999. *(Valor)*

DePaola, Tomie. *La leyenda de la flor «el conejo»* (The legend of the flower "bluebonnet"). New York: Putnam, 1989. *(Sacrificio, valor)*

Haggerty, Mary Elizabeth. *Una grieta en la pared* (A crack in the wall). New York: Lee & Low, 1993. *(Temor)*

Martinez, Alejandra Cruz. *La mujer que brillaba aún más que el sol* (The woman who outshone the sun). San Francisco: Children's Book Press, 1991. *(Prejuicio)*

Parke, Marilyn, & Sharon Panik. *Un cuento de Quetzalcóatl acerca del juego de pelota* (A Quetzalcóatl tale of the ball game). Carthage, IL: Fearon Teacher Aids, 1992. *(Solución de problema, perseverancia)*

Parke, Marilyn, & Sharon Panik. *Un cuento de Quetzalcóatl acerca del maíz* (A Quetzalcóatl tale of the corn). Carthage, IL: Fearon Teacher Aids, 1992. *(Solución de problema, perseverancia)*

Scholes, Katherine. *Tiempo de paz* (Peace begins with you). Editorial Origen, S. A. de C. V., Roberto Gayol 1219, Colonia del Valle, Mexico, D. F. C. P. 03100. *(Amistad, solución de problema)*

Steadman, Ralph. *El puente* (The bridge). Artes Gráficas, Ibarra, S. A., 1972. *(Amistad, solución de problema)*

Tabor, Nancy Maria Grande. *Somos un arco iris* (We are a rainbow). Watertown, MA: Charlesbridge, 1995. *(Auto-estima)*

Resources for Teachers and Parents

Borba, Michele, & Craig Borba. *Self-Esteem: A Classroom Affair, 101 Ways to Help Children Like Themselves.* San Francisco: HarperSanFrancisco, [1978] 1993.

Curwin, Richard L., & Allen N. Mendler. *Discipline with Dignity.* Alexandria, VA: Association for Supervision and Curriculum Development, 1988.

Dreikurs, Rudolph, & Loren Grey. *New Approach to Discipline: Logical Consequences.* New York: Plume, 1993.

Dreikurs, Rudolph, Bernice Bronia Grunwald, & Floy C. Pepper. *Maintaining Sanity in the Classroom: Classroom Management Techniques,* 2d ed. Philadelphia, PA: 1998.

Glasser, William. *Schools without Failure.* New York: Harper & Row, 1969.

Glasser, William. *The Quality School Teacher.* New York: HarperCollins, 1993.

Good, Perry E. *In Pursuit of Happiness: Knowing What You Want, Getting What You Need.* Chapel Hill, NC: New View, 1987.

Gootman, Marilyn E. *The Loving Parents' Guide to Discipline: How to Teach Your Child to Behave—With Kindness, Understanding, and Respect.* New York: Berkeley Publishing Group, 2000.

Kreidler, William J., & Sandy Tsubokawa Whittall. *Early Childhood Adventures in Peacemaking: A Conflict Resolution Guide for Early Childhood Educators,* 2d ed. Cambridge, MA: Educators for Social Responsibility, and Boston: Work/Family Directions, 1999.

Levin, Diane E. *Teaching Young Children in Violent Times: Building a Peaceable Classroom.* Cambridge, MA: Educators for Social Responsibility, 1994.

Nelsen, Jane, Lynn Lott, & H. Stephen Glenn. *Positive Discipline, A-Z, from Toddler to Teens,* 2d ed. Roseville, CA: Prima, 1987.

Pirtle, Sarah. *Linking Up!* Cambridge, MA: Educators for Social Responsibility, 1998.

Styles, Donna. *Class Meetings.* Markham, ONT: Pembroke Publishers, 2001. (Distributed by Stenhouse Publishers, Portland, ME)

Sullo, Robert. *Teach Them to Be Happy.* Chapel Hill, NC: New View, 1993.

Early years are learning years

Become a member of NAEYC, and help make them count!

Just as you help young children learn and grow, the National Association for the Education of Young Children—your professional organization—supports you in the work you love. NAEYC is the world's largest early childhood education organization, with a national network of local, state, and regional Affiliates. We are more than 100,000 members working together to bring high-quality early learning opportunities to all children from birth through age eight.

Since 1926, NAEYC has provided educational services and resources for people working with children, including:

• *Young Children*, the award-winning journal (six issues a year) for early childhood educators

• **Books, posters, brochures, and videos** to support your work with young children and families

• **The NAEYC Annual Conference**, which brings tens of thousands of people together from across the country and around the world to share their expertise and ideas on the education of young children

• **Insurance plans** for members and programs

• **A voluntary accreditation system** to help programs reach national standards for high-quality early childhood education

• **Young Children International** to promote global communication and information exchanges

• **www.naeyc.org**—a dynamic Website with up-to-date information on all of our services and resources

To join NAEYC

For a list of membership benefits and options or to join NAEYC online, visit **www.naeyc.org/membership**. Or you can mail this form to us.

(Membership must be for an individual, not a center or school.)

Name _____

Address_____

City_____ State_____ ZIP_____

E-mail _____

Phone (H)_____ (W) _____

❏ New member   ❏ Renewal ID # _____

Affiliate name/number _____

To determine your dues, you must visit www.naeyc.org/membership or call 800-424-2460, ext. 2002.

Indicate your payment option

❏ VISA   ❏ MasterCard

Card # _____Exp. date_____

Cardholder's name _____

Signature _____

Note: By joining NAEYC you also become a member of your state and local Affiliates.

Send this form and your payment to

NAEYC, PO Box 97156, Washington, DC 20009-7156